Brodie Murray, a proud Wamba Wamba and Ngarrindjeri man, is a playwright and performer committed to sharing the survival stories of Victorian Aboriginal communities. His plays, including *Soul of Possum*, *The Whisper* and *Billy's Choice*, have garnered accolades including the 2021 Melbourne Fringe Best Emerging Indigenous Artist Award.

Tom Molyneux, a Gunditjmara man, is a versatile creative professional based on Wadawurrung Country in Djilang (Geelong). He is recognised for his riveting performances in works such as *The Mission*, which he wrote and toured nationally and which earned him the 2023 Green Room Award for Best Performer (Independent Theatre).

Tracey Rigney, a Wotjobaluk and Ngarrindjeri woman, is an acclaimed storyteller and filmmaker whose work spans theatre and film, with notable credits including the play *Belonging* and the documentary 'Endangered'.

Together, these artists contribute to a deeper understanding and appreciation of First Nations history, culture and contemporary issues through their compelling and diverse artistic practices.

WAS AND WILL BE

A FIRST NATIONS ANTHOLOGY BY
TRACEY RIGNEY
BRODIE MURRAY
& TOM MOLYNEUX

CURRENCY PRESS
The performing arts publisher

First published in 2024
by Currency Press Pty Ltd,
Gadigal Land, Suite 310, 46–56 Kippax Street, Surry Hills, NSW 2010, Australia
enquiries@currency.com.au
www.currency.com.au

Copyright: *Was And Will Be: A First Nations Anthology* © Tracey Rigney, Brodie Murray and Thomas Molyneux; Teachers' notes © Nick Waxman

COPYING FOR EDUCATIONAL PURPOSES

The Australian *Copyright Act 1968* [Act] allows a maximum of one chapter or 10% of this book, whichever is the greater, to be copied by any educational institution for its educational purposes provided that that educational institution [or the body that administers it] has given a remuneration notice to Copyright Agency [CA] under the Act.

For details of the CA licence for educational institutions contact CA, 12 / 66 Goulburn Street, Sydney, NSW, 2000; tel: within Australia 1800 066 844 toll free; outside Australia 61 2 9394 7600; fax: 61 2 9394 7601; memberservices@copyright.com.au

COPYING FOR OTHER PURPOSES

Except as permitted under the Act, for example a fair dealing for the purposes of study, research, criticism or review, no part of this book may be reproduced, stored in a retrieval system, or transmitted in any form or by any means without prior written permission. All enquiries should be made to the publisher at the address above.

Any performance or public reading of *Was and Will Be* is forbidden unless a licence has been received from the authors' agent. The purchase of this book in no way gives the purchaser the right to perform the play in public, whether by means of a staged production or a reading. All applications for public performance should be addressed to David Spicer Productions, PO Box 2280, Rose Bay North, NSW 2030 Australia; 02 9371 8458; david@davidspicer.com

No part of this book may be used or reproduced in any manner for the purpose of training artificial intelligence technologies or systems without the express written permission of the author and the publisher.

Typeset by Currency Press.

Cover artwork and design by Steve Parker. Steve is a descendant from Boonwurrung, Yorta Yorta and Erub (TSI) people and is from Millowl (known as Phillip Island).

All photographs within the text are taken by Jacob McCormack at Frankston Arts Centre and Haileybury College in the premiere production, 2024.

Currency Press acknowledges the Traditional Owners of the Country on which we live and work. We pay our respects to all Aboriginal and Torres Strait Islander Elders, past and present.

 A catalogue record for this book is available from the National Library of Australia

Contents

About the Project	ix
Utilising This Anthology	x
Foreword by Jane Harrison	xii
THE SCRIPTS	1
Tracey Rigney	3
CMT (Culturally modified tree)	4
My Reincarnation	5
Life-long Friend	6
Conversation with Daughter	7
Guide	9
Wotjobaluk Stories Part I	10
Wotjobaluk Stories Part II	12
Wotjobaluk Stories Part III	14
United We Fall	17
What Best Friends Do ...	19
The Meeting	20
Pure Heart	22
The Hood	24
Fan (Stan)	27

January 26: Haiku	28
When We Caste Our Eyes at Her: Haiku	28
Referendum 2023: Haiku	28
Tom Molyneux	29
Colours	30
Concrete	32
Papa	33
Echoes	37
Elders' Eyes	43
Being Well	45
Brodie Murray	47
My River Country	48
Yidaki/Didgeridoo	52
The Marngrook	53
Good Works	55
Representation	56
Reflections 1	57
Reflections 2	57
Reflections 3	57
TEACHERS' NOTES	73
CMT (Culturally modified tree)	74
My Reincarnation	75
Life-long Friend	76

Conversation with Daughter	77
Guide	78
Wotjobaluk Stories	79
United We Fall	81
What Best Friends Do ...	82
The Meeting	84
Pure Heart	85
The Hood	86
Fan (Stan)	88
Three Haikus	89
Colours	90
Concrete	92
Papa	94
Echoes	96
Elders' Eyes	97
Being Well	98
My River Country	99
Yidaki/Didgeridoo	101
The Marngrook	102
Good Works	104
Representation	105
Three Reflections	106

About the Project

This anthology was conceived and developed by Nick Waxman (pictured above) who provided additional creative resources and education notes for the work. Nick is a writer, educator and performer from Naarm. Nick would like to thank these artists for their generous contributions to this work.

Thank you to Frankston City Council, Jane Harrison, Glenn Shea, Anthony Crowley, Dr Danielle Hradsky, Kelly McConville, Andrew Byrne, Haileybury, Steve Parker and Drama Victoria for their support of this project.

Utilising This Anthology

Purpose and Access
This anthology, crafted with contributions from three First Nations artists—Tracey Rigney, Brodie Murray and Tom Molyneux—serves as a repository of open scripts, offering versatile narratives that span monologues, dialogues, choruses and dynamic movement sequences. This collection is specifically designed to be accessible and enriching for both Indigenous and non-Indigenous actors, creatives, educators, students and theatre enthusiasts.

Versatility and Adaptability
The scripts are inherently flexible, allowing for varied interpretations and adaptations to suit different group sizes and settings—from a duo to a classroom of thirty or a cast of 100. Whether in educational environments, theatrical productions, or informal readings, you are encouraged to delve into the scripts, exploring the profound themes and stories embedded within them. Scenes can be presented in any order unless specified.

Engagement and Exploration
Readers are urged to engage with the material actively by reading the scripts, exploring accompanying resources and conducting further research to deepen their understanding of the themes. This approach not only enriches your experience but also enhances your appreciation and respect for First Nations narratives.

Creative Freedom
The anthology champions creative freedom, encouraging users to interpret and present the works in ways that resonate most profoundly with their personal or collective experiences. This flexibility supports a wide range of expressive possibilities, from traditional performances to more innovative, experimental forms of theatre.

Cultural Reflection and Education
Above all, this anthology aims to foster a reflective and educational space where individuals can connect with, reflect upon and celebrate the rich cultural heritage of Victorian First Nations peoples. It is a tool for cultural engagement and learning, promoting a broader understanding and appreciation of Indigenous stories and traditions.

Original production
Was And Will Be was first produced at Frankston Arts Centre and Haileybury on 21 August 2024, directed by Nicole Smith, Candice Anderson, Emma Maggio and Nick Waxman.

Foreword

Stories make us human and First Nations people have used stories to impart culture, language and knowledge for millennia. Stories are to be shared and they help us engender empathy and understanding. When we delve into stories our shared humanity comes to the fore. As First Nations people we are unique but as humans we can share emotions, beliefs and values. These talented and generous storytellers have created scenes that allow you to walk in our shoes for a moment in time and to embody these narratives. This is a rare and special opportunity and a gift that will inform you for a lifetime. Use this material with respect but also give yourselves permission to explore, experiment and connect.

Jane Harrison, playwright
Muruwari

The Scripts

Tracey Rigney
Wotjobaluk and Ngarrindjeri

Embark on a journey into the poignant and powerful scripts of Tracey Rigney, a distinguished Wotjobaluk and Ngarrindjeri woman from Victoria, acclaimed for her diverse contributions to film, television and theatre. Tracey's work, deeply anchored in her Indigenous heritage, vividly captures the essence of human experiences, cultural identity and personal transformations through evocative narratives and vibrant characters.

Tracey would like to acknowledge that the following scripts were written on Wotjobaluk Country.

CMT (Culturally Modified Tree)

Some of us have these markings on us.
These special scars.
We were the chosen ones
From those who lived before
From those who spoke different languages
From those who sang different songs
And danced, kicking up the dirt with their bare feet
Those who honoured the Country
The animals
The water
The sky
Those who always took what was necessary
And made sure there was enough
Those who used fire to manage the landscape
And made sure the water ran clear
Some of us who still stand today
See a new generation of these old people
We thought they wouldn't make it
Wouldn't survive
But they did
Some of us who still stand today
Are losing our markings
Are losing our ability
To remain in this landscape
But we know
These new generations of people
Are choosing others like me to mark
These special scars.

My Reincarnation

Here I am.
In the middle of the cold desert again.
Where my mind plays tricks on me and I think that I see you my love
But just like a mirage you're not really there
So I stand alone in this barren landscape,
Freezing cold and wishing to find a real place to belong
So I take a couple of steps and realise that I've come to be on the edge of a cliff, looking out over a turbulent sea
I think I see you again my love.
You're microscopic in size, and at the base of the cliff bobbing up and down like floating debris
Waving your arms about, looking up at me.
I wish for you to be rescued by a passing whale,
So you can ride it out to the horizon and beyond
So you can ride it to be with your Ancestors, at the edge of the dark cloud, where only the light shines
But then you fade beneath the water
With a smile on your face
I've never seen you smile like that before?
And then the waves vanish and the ocean settles
And I find myself alone again
In the cemetery standing before your unmarked grave
Crying my eyes out
And then I wake up.

Life-long Friend

Grief visited me when I was four
They told me they were a new friend.
We played hide and seek in the house.
A house in inner Melbourne suburbia
I hid so well that grief couldn't find me for a long time
They finally found me hiding in my old bassinet in the back room
I love hiding in there when I play with my brothers.
We then went outside and I climbed the apricot tree
Grief followed me up and we sat there looking around the backyard
I like being up in high places.
I showed the shed where I climbed one time following my brothers
I got stuck there and my dad climbed up to get me down
I remember he had hairy arms.
And a Bugs Bunny tattoo.
An apricot fell to the ground.
We watched it fall.
I told grief that I don't eat apricots
I then pointed to a corner of the backyard where my brothers tried to make a swimming pool
I don't know where my mum is right now, I said to grief.
Grief asked me where my dad was.
I said he's in the kitchen making me toast.
Grief thanked me for playing.
Grief climbed down and picked up the fallen apricot
They opened up the apricot and removed a seed.
Grief handed it to me and said they will return again when the seed grows.
I put the seed inside my heart.
I now carry an orchard in there.

Conversation with Daughter

Were you alive before the internet?
Yes, yes I was.
I come from the olden days / dark ages / ancient times where:
Before mobile phones
Telephones were the only way to communicate by speaking
We had one that you dialled and it was on the wall
Fax machines could send words and pictures
Revolutionary!
I learned to type on a typewriter
Yes the machine before computers
Don't know what it is—look it up
Computers were just coming in to schools
They had floppy disks before there were hard disks
USB sticks and now there are clouds online
We had no laptops back then
And to get online we had to dial up, no wifi
Took ages and made weird electronic noises
Before game consoles
We used to go down to the local cafe and play the pinnies
Your uncle was the best and his name was always on top as highest scorer
We spent whole days down there eating hot chips and dim sims
Drinking mello yello
Eating one and two cent lollies
We never had a car
We walked everywhere
Or rode our push bikes
We didn't wear helmets—but you have to!
We popped monos and rode with no hands
We'd spend whole days swimming in the river
Hanging bombs off the bridge
Playing around the world on the rope hanging from the tree
We bounced on trampolines that had no netting
We were rough
We were tough

We spent years playing outside

Wearing hand-me-downs
Living in our imaginations
Making up our own fun
Us Country kids
Childhood only seemed like yesterday
Where did the time go?
Things have changed
But somehow I still feel the same

Guide

Let me take you on a journey
Past
Present
Future
Do you see my hand?
The Feather?
The White feather?
A symbol
My love for you
Take it
It's yours
And come with me
I will help guide the way
Don't mind the darkness
My voice
Like a beacon
The moon in the night
The sun in the day
My energy is strong now
Like nature
Cyclonic winds
The ocean—the sea
Like gravity
It's time
All you have to do is take
A step—A leap
Of faith
Trust
In
This
Me
Us

Wotjobaluk Stories: A trilogy as told by Tracey Rigney
Part I: The Journey of Barringgi Gadyin

The Barringgi Gadyin is a unique river system
In the state now known as Victoria
The river begins in the mountains
A cooler climate
Unfamiliar Country
Another culture
Its journey begins there in the east
And then it flows west
It meanders and winds then turns
Travelling north
It flows inland
Not into a sea or ocean like the rest
Instead it meets a large freshwater lake
Nestled in sandhill Country
This is Gurru
It then travels along a deep creek line
Rich with culturally modified trees
Rich with earth ovens
Rich with scatter sites
This is Kromeluk
Flows from Barringgi Gadyin move from this creek line
North towards another freshwater lake
This is Ngelbakutya
The river red gums are stunning
This wetland is world heritage listed
Mallee terrain
Barringgi Gadyin then continues on to the small teardrop lakes
And wetlands far beyond
Gurru barely gets water these days
Kromeluk is lucky to have a puddle
Ngelbakutya has been empty for decades
These names
Wergaia language
Is what the Wotjobaluk called these places

Their songlines are linked to this unique river system
Ancient stories
Older than time itself

Pronunication guide
Barringgi Gadyin *Bar-ring-ghee Gad-jun*
Gurru *Gu-roo*
Kromeluk *Krom-mul-luck*
Ngelbakutya *Nyell-buck-ut-cha*
Wergaia *Wurr-guy-ya*
Wotjobaluk *Watch-a-bal-luck*

Wotjobaluk Stories: A trilogy as told by Tracey Rigney
Part II: The Legacy of Wotjobaluk Elders

A Wotjobaluk man
Told me many stories
He told me how he remembered when
The Barringgi Gadyin was clear
He could see the fish swimming
He used to catch eels in there
They don't live in there today
One time he showed me where he was born
Among the Beal trees
The River red gums
On the banks of the Barringgi Gadyin
I saw the remains of a clay mud hut
Its walls were the shape of a circle
But then I could see a gap
This was the door entrance
His birth place
Not far from Ebenezer Mission
Where his people survived
He told me the rising land on which the Mission stands
Was ceremonial ground for corroborees
An important meeting place to the Wotjobaluk
The European man who 'owned the land'
Knew this and told the Missionaries from Moravia
That's how the land was chosen
The Mission saved Wotjobaluk lives
But destroyed Wotjobaluk culture
This European man also participated in the elimination
Of Wotjobaluk people
There's a street named after him
In Dimboola a nearby town
Would you believe me if I told you I live on it
This European man took a 'lonely' boy in this one time
The story goes this European man
Was responsible for his mum's 'departure'

This Wotjobaluk boy
Known as Willie Wimmera
This boy first went to Naarm
Far from home
Then travelled by boat
Over vast seas and oceans
Across the world
Even further from home
He was only eleven
Still a boy
Just a child
He was Christianised
The Europeans were proud of his conversion
He was an exemplar
They wanted to bring him back home
To convert other Wotjobaluk
To Christianise others like the Wotjobaluk
They had a role for him
But he got sick
Maybe
Really
He
Was
Home sick?
The boy returned to spirit
He is buried in Reading, England
This Wotjobaluk boy
He remains over there
To this day

Pronunication guide
Beal *Be-ull*
Naarm *Narm*

Wotjobaluk Stories: A trilogy as told by Tracey Rigney
Part III: Continuity and Change

The Wotjobaluk man
Also told me about his Great Grandfather
A man who helped find the lost Duff children
Near Dyurrite
It's a beautiful mountain
In 1864 he helped track them
Even after the rains washed away the kids' tracks
In the middle of winter
In thick dense scrub
He helped find them
Alive
The *Lost in the Bush* story
On Jardwajdali Country
His Great Grandfather also
Travelled to England
He played cricket
He could run backwards fast
He could deflect up to four cricket balls
Being thrown at him
All at once
With his shield and waddy
And never be hit
The first 'Australian team' 1868
This Wotjobaluk man
Showed me out on Country
How he made boomerangs
He'd get me to paint them
As I sat at his feet
As a little girl
And he would tell me many stories
Over and over
And over again
About his Country
About his culture

About his life
Like when he was four or five
His Elders took him out bush
Among the banksias
Among the acacias
The variety of eucalypts
And desert critters
Large and small
They left him there
He waited
And waited some more
He was scared
All alone
Tears flowed
Then a thought came
Like a message from the Dreaming
They're trying to teach me something?
And just like his Great Grandfather
He followed their tracks
Tracking his way
Their footprints led him to them
They were waiting on the edge of the bush
And celebrated his lesson
He passed with flying colours
This Wotjobaluk man
Could speak Wergaia fluently as a child
But would get the strap at school
He was forced to speak English
Little by little
The amount of his vocabulary
Became limited
This Wotjobaluk man
Spent the final ten years of his life
Fighting for his people
His Country
His culture
And in 2005

Wotjobaluk people
Won Native Title recognition
In the eyes of the European's ways
The first to do so in what is known as South-Eastern Australia
BUT
His body could no longer house his warrior spirit
This returned World War Two soldier
He closed his eyes one last time
He took his final inhale
And exhale
So he could journey to the Dreaming
Where Willie Wimmera went before him
Where those who dwelled on the Mission returned to
Where those Wotjobaluk
Who met the fate of European weapons
Crossed over to
He transitioned
Before the Native Title consent determination
His life mattered
His life had impact
His legacy remains
This Wotjobaluk man
Was my Grandfather
And is the reason
I tell stories.

Pronunication guide
Dyurrite *Jurr-right*
Jardwajdali *Jar-da-wa-jar-lee*
Waddy *Wod-dee*

United We Fall

She is always up for fun
She gets so excited over the little things
She has tonnes of energy
I used to forget about her
Over the years I neglected her
Even took her for granted
I softly said to her
Those days are gone
She does matter to me
I hug her often
She feels safe in my arms
I make sure we have lots of laughs
Be silly and have fun!
We pack the bag
Skates
Check
Wrist guards
Check
Knee pads
Check
Elbow pads
Check
Helmet
Check
Drink bottle full of water check
We arrive and gear up
Then it's time
Music pumping
We smile
We laugh
We fall
We get up
We laugh some more
We fall again
We glide

We transition
Each new trick is a slow burn
A physical challenge
More mental perhaps
We roll
We skate
We sticky skate
We backwards skate
We feel alive
We lose track of time
Nothing matters in this moment
Nothing except us
Absolute freedom
Pure joy
I love her
I love us
We are one
My inner child and me

What Best Friends Do …

Never lie to each other—only for each other and especially to liars
Spend an entire day at school—only to get home and text each other for the rest of the day and night until school the next day.
Go to the toilet together …
And if necessary hand each other toilet paper if there's none in there (Yes I have a square, a square to spare)
Wear similar clothes when you don't mean to—BFF vibes are real
Cry together during animated shows (the film *The Wild Robot* sob sob sob)
Laugh together at the same things with tears flowing—tears gotta flow otherwise it's not really that funny (and you gotta gasp for air)
Make a tartan hippopotamus toy—so their bestie doesn't fail textiles—true story
Walk the cross-Country track together—because running long distance sucks—another true story
Start each other's sentences as well as finish them—it's like two minds are one with your bestie
Listen to the same music for hours on end and lose track of time
But realise as an adult that time is the most precious thing
Have sleepovers and not really sleep
Share secrets that will go to each other's graves
Share each other's dreams
Share each other's fears
Be a sympathetic ear with no judgement—but judge the hell out of mean people
Always be there for each other—except when sick or something serious like a concert
Fight for each other—but never with each other
Even when apart by distance—the closeness remains
Grow together—not apart
I love my biological family … but my BFF is my logical family
Because in the end, best friends are the family we choose

The Meeting

I'd like to acknowledge the traditional owners of the lands that we are gathered upon today and pay my respects to Ancestors and Elders past and present. Sovereignty was never ceded, always was, always will be. Okay let's start the meeting. Present. Apologies.
Why?
Why what?
Acknowledge?
Because it's a meeting.
But why?
You're here. I'm here. They're here. We're all here. Meeting.
About what?
Didn't you get the agenda?
What agenda?
For the meeting?
This meeting?
Yes the one you're present at.
Is this a meeting or an acknowledgement?
Yes this is a meeting and yes that was an acknowledgement
Are you present or an apology
Apologise for what?
The meeting
Why?
I'm not sorry
I'm not asking if you're sorry
Why should we be sorry?
I'm sorry I'm not understanding you?
Why be sorry?
Look if you don't want to be here
We're here now—we can't change that
I apologise
For what?
For the meeting
So are you an apology?
I'm not an apology
Are you sorry?

Sorry?
Sorry?
Sorry?
Sorry?
Sorry?
Sorry?
Sorry?
Sorry!
Yes
I
Am.
You should be too!
Present or apology?

Pure Heart

Please, for the love of Bunjil don't idolise the girls you watch online
They are showing you something that isn't real
Okay sure I write stories that aren't real either—good point
But I'm not shoving products down your throat so you annoy your parents to buy them
I know you don't wanna hear this but everything in life isn't about make-up and fashion
Just hear me out and stop crossing your arms and rolling your eyes
It's about who you are on the inside
Your heart—your essence
I know that sounds boring—but it's the truth
Of course I tell the truth
Lies only lead to more lies
Like when you told me you lost a tooth the other day and showed me a small white malformed pebble
In the hope I would put it out for the tooth fairy?
Oh you're quiet now?
Yes I digress
Fame and fortune is an unhealthy lifestyle
Please don't argue with me on this point
It's such a superficial life
What I mean is that people are so fake
They are so shallow
They don't care about anything in life except their image and their brand
If you were to pass these people on the street
They wouldn't even give you a look
They wouldn't even say hello
They'd look at you and shriek trying to run away from you in their expensive but poor taste heels
While trying to not let their make-up run out of fear you would see actual
Oh I can't bear to say this
Pimples and blotchy skin!
Please keep your natural features!

Please don't get fake lips
Fake cheeks
Fake anything!!!
You are beautiful as your real and natural self.
When you see yourself in any reflection
Know that you are looking at the greatest love of your life YOU!
I urge you!
Please do not grow up to be like any of these people!
It doesn't matter what size you are, what shape you are, what clothes you wear, what colour your hair is, what colour your skin is, what you look like
We are the same inside
But what sets us apart is how genuine and kind the heart is
Make sure yours is—always!
Follow your heart and trust in the feelings it gives you
This is your intuition
You can't go wrong when you are in tune with it
Now go for a bounce on the trampoline or something.
Love you!
And no you can't take my phone with you …

The Hood

Like an invisible shadow
Something was missing
This parade of one
Trudging through puddled streets
A rippled half smile reflected back
This life
Is there more to this life?
I've lived
I've loved
I've lost
Experiences
Is that why we're here?
In the physical?
To materialise?
To manifest?
Shifting energies?
A string of moments
Lessons and memories
Mistakes and forgiveness
Learning to love
Learning to let go
Learning to trust
Learning to be better
And do better
Why do so many of us suffer?
Ravaged by war?
Famine?
Poverty?
Born one minute
Gone the next?
On a crowded tram
Alone
Isolated
There's so many more of you
You don't even notice

I hear your languages
I observe your etiquette
Perhaps it's not about becoming?
Rather unbecoming
The person
The being
Always been
Trying on personalities
Like masks
Experimenting with bad habits
Like costumes
Uttering vernaculars
Like wearing shades of lipsticks
I like it here
It's fun
But empty
Always felt an inkling
Maybe one day
But never really knew
Or was never really that brave
Home
On Country
Culture
Connected
And then
I discovered you
A hidden treasure
Like a missing jigsaw piece
I dreamed you into existence
And here you are
An absolute dream
My love for you is infinite
You're my greatest teacher
The best medicine
I never knew who I truly was
Or what I was capable of
Until you arrived

Is this what fulfillment is?
Is this what life is all about?
One thing I know is
You give my life meaning
And purpose
Like never before

Fan (Stan)

Is it a Scorpio trait?
Obsess Possess
Here I must confess
I heard you
I saw you
You mesmerised me
Left an imprint
Moved my spirit
The way you sang
The way you danced
The way you inspire
Your fashion
Your existence made an impact
In a myriad of ways
Music was otherworldly for you
You received songs
A conduit
Your music has been the only constant in my life
Since childhood. Youth. Adulthood
The highest ups. The deepest lows
My evolution
You are the soundtrack to my life
Always your fangirl

January 26: Haiku

Hot breeze where tribes thrive
Ships invaded a coastline
Monsters are real

When We Caste Our Eyes at Her: Haiku

What part of her is
Aboriginal to us
Her middle finger?

Referendum 2023: Haiku

Our nation voted
No doesn't define their race
Reflects who we are

Tom Molyneux
Gunditjmara

Explore the compelling and evocative theatre works of Tom Molyneux, a proud Gunditjmara man. With a keen eye for storytelling and a deep connection to his heritage, Tom's works resonate with authenticity, emotional depth and cultural richness. These scripts delve into themes such as identity, connection to Country, intergenerational trauma and the enduring spirit of First Nations resilience.

Tom would like to acknowledge that the following scripts were written on Gunditjmara and Wadawurrung Country.

Colours

Look at these cliffs
Layers of colour
Of time
Of stories
Baked into the earth.

Now that the jagged edges have come apart,
Washed, and split, and sawed by the tides,
The landslides,
The shoreline that keeps shifting;
Slightly different now than what the Ancestors stared at,
And theirs was different to their Ancestors too …
But while it moves, the layers keep on building.
You can see it all in sharp relief
Gorgeous yellow
Blurring all the way into rich, berry-like red,
There's white
And grey
And bits of blue.
A spectrum of colour to keep returning to,
To trade
Or smear on your body
In war
Or in ceremony.
A little bit of water is all it takes
To transform this coloured cliff
Into paint.
Both paint and canvas.
The cliff now holds stories
And menus,
Warnings
And maps.

Maps.
They're different now.
Once used for survival, for education, or planning your travel—

An ancient Lonely Planet guide.
New maps, still using colours, but full of new boundaries.
This rich, berry-like, red line
Now used to delineate
To alienate
To exclude
To possess, own and control.

Who knew it was as easy
As painting a rich, berry-like red line.

A young man
Presses his palm against the cliff
Gratefully removing a small chunk of red
Grinding it gently on a stone, with fresh salty water.
His finger smears the chalky, rich, berry-like red across his face.
Line after line.
He is ready.

Concrete

Actors are positioned in a semicircle. One begins pounding the earth, in a slow, rhythmic fashion.

After some time, a second begins pounding the earth, in a distinct counter-rhythm. A third then commences another rhythm. And so on, with other performers.

Whilst it may not be immediately clear, the beat is not only percussive— it should become apparent that these performers have the intention to dig through an impossibly hard surface, without success.

The effect should be like vehicle indicators stopped at traffic lights, coming in and out of sync with each other. The more rhythms the better.

One performer, preferably a woman, may at one point change from beating the earth, to beating her skull, reminiscent of intense grief.

Another performer, preferably a man, may do likewise at another point during the rhythm, but beating his chest.

The pounding rises to a crescendo—and then suddenly cuts out.

We could be doing this for another thousand years, and still not find Country.

Papa

I hold his hand
And look into his eyes.
Or rather, behind his eyes.
The man that was—
Who had such adventures
Was a larrikin
Always ready with a lame joke
Or a corny saying
Like: 'Ever been to India? Well get it In-to-ya'
'If I don't see you through the week, I'll see you through the window' ...
Hmm
Now those eyes
Don't seem to see much
Everything is slower
And though he's surrounded with kindness
This aged care centre is a far cry from open Country
And dementia turns his sharp storytelling
Into a
Muddled
Faded
Obscured
Memory.

Memory with a question mark.

There is something to be said
For the painful memories becoming less clear.
Or am I projecting that?
I'm sure he didn't even have memories
Of being taken at the age of one
From his father,
His seven siblings,
His happy little baby life
And put into a 'baby's home'.
Hard to imagine they had such places ...
But growing up with an unknown hole in your heart,

Being given a new, adopted surname,
Suddenly an 'only child'
Going to church,
Sleeping out the back of your new parents' home, not in the guest room.
Of course not.
Seeing a man with skin like yours in the crowd at the football, calling your name, 'Bobby! Bobby!', being whisked away from this man quick smart, 'How did he know my name?', 'Let's not speak of this again'.
The man keeps appearing,
Across the road from the school at lunchtime,
This man with a limp, a prosthetic leg,
He looks so familiar …
And yet, so unknown.

One day, the limping man stops appearing.
It's not til much later
That the truth comes out.
Coroner's reports. Police cells. Hush hush.
'Let's not speak of this again.'

Six-year-old me
Sits on the back porch with Papa.
He's smuggled me a choc ice from the back freezer, his secret stash that Grandma doesn't know about.
'Papa, do you have any brothers and sisters?'
I ask it innocently enough, but he still flinches
'Yeah, quite a few, but we didn't grow up together.'
'I wish I didn't have to grow up with my brothers …'
'Don't say that.'
His tone is hard. Flinty. Unlike him.
I listen. And reflect.

Fast forward.
We're driving to an aged care centre.
He doesn't want to go. Of course he doesn't.
It's a lucid moment, amongst the dementia.
No-one wants to be institutionalised.

Fragments of memory.
Finally hugging your brother, tears rolling into his biceps.
Learning your real name.
Having two kids of your own, to pass your stories down to.
Heart holes being filled.
Slowly.

Grandkids.
Choc ice.
Flowers.
Funerals.
Waking up in a strange bed.
What's this machine?
How do I get home from here?
Escape.
Taxi.
No money to pay.
Back to the strange room.
Grandson visiting. What's his name again?
Rinse.
Repeat.
Rinse.
Repeat.
…
I stare into those eyes
And grip his hand.
Quietly sure it's the last time.
'Thanks Papa.'
Hm?
'If I don't see you through the week, I'll see you through the window.'

I'm overseas.
The call comes through.
It's not a shock, but still a gut punch.
I walk to the beach, to try to remember.
Grateful for even the fragments of memory
And the lessons
And the stories

And the example
Of healing yourself.
Even when it's painful.
Memories that last, even when your own have disappeared.
Thanks Papa.

Echoes

We stand on the beach
Markers of time
Of place
Of stone
Of sand
And the metronome of the tide.
It has beat these shores
For years
For decades
For millennia.
How many others have stood like we are now
Observing and remembering
My Ancestors.
Your Ancestors.
Those waves have seen some things …

What do you call a place like this
Which has seen such stories,
Ceremony /
Bloodshed /
Celebration /
Mourning /
Contest /
Conflict /
Conquest.

Sacred?
Scarred.
…
Did you feel that gust of wind?
It's freezing!
Ssh, we're honouring.
But it's a little creepy don't you think?
Just take your shoes off and feel the sand between your toes.
I can't feel my toes—
Ssh!

Blood has been spilled on this sand.
…
Did you know
30,000 years ago
Four giants arrived here
They moved off to find other places to live
But one,
Called Budj Bim,
Laid down
His head protruding up was visible from a great distance—
Looks like a hill to me—
'Budj Bim'—it means 'high head'.
I think I've found my new nickname for you …

Then one day
He overheated
Sat up
Spitting out his teeth
Huge chunks of scoria
Soaring out across Gunditjmara Country.
Ancestors watching
Lava flowing
Landscapes changing
Before their very eyes.
You wouldn't forget a thing like that!

The story goes that Budj Bim,
Knowing he needed to cool down,
Dragged himself down towards the ocean to cool off
And his legs were so heavy
That he left these lava tubes scarring the surface of Country behind him.

    They stare at the ocean.

Well I'm sure he had no trouble cooling down here. Far out it's cold! Sssssh!
  …

So why do they call this place 'Convincing Ground'?
Yeah I was wondering that too.
Such a weird name …
The story goes:
There was a whale—
When was this?
Ages ago
When this place was still part of New South Wales
Ironic …
That's what the newcomers called it anyway.
So there was a whale?
Yep, a beached one.
Lots of whales up and down this coast
Big guy, lost his way
Or escaped the whalers maybe?
The stranding was just the start of the story though
Like all the whales before him
His carcass was valuable
Lots of food
And skin
And blubber.
The *kilcarer gunditj* had seen many like it before
And got to work
Proud of what they would be able to provide for their community.
But this whale was different
Or rather, the beach was different now.
The Henty family
And their workers
Had established a settlement nearby
Turning temporary whaling stations
Into something more … permanent.
It's not clear who
But some whalers took their opportunity
They had laid their claim to whales in the open ocean
And now this one on the beach would be theirs too.
Said one whaler to his mate:
'We must convince them. About whose whale this is.'

The subtext:
'And also whose land this is.'
But they were no master debaters
Convincing with rational argument,
Rather their language of choice was
Gunpowder
Bullets
Rifles, hastily fetched from their huts.
The *kilcarer gunditj* men fought
With what weapons they had
But even 60 men—
Some say 200—
Were no match for this firepower.

Rifles aren't a native species on this continent.

All but two were killed
In cold blood
And then their blood ran cold
on *this* beach.

The whalers
Used to gruesome work
Believed their job was done.
They had 'convinced' the locals of their rights to the whale, and the beach.
But it didn't stop.
They kept convincing.
It was addictive.

These Hentys
Who had landed in Western Australia first
And were 'gifted' 34,000 acres of Noongar Country
For their sheep—
Who clearly needed their space!
But the soil wasn't to their liking
(Or something like that)
So they packed it in

And sailed to Tassie—
Ahem, at that time, Van Diemen's Land—
lutruwita
To breed their sheep there
Only to find there were no more parcels of free land being given out
And so
Despite knowing it was illegal
to settle there yet
They knew it looked good
And decided to chance their arm
In Western Victoria—
Ahem, at that time, New South Wales—
Gunditjmara Country
Expanding their 'pastures'
Away from the prying eyes of the 'authorities'
Until they were too big
Too established
Too wealthy
For the land to be taken back off them.

Australia's biggest 'Convincers'.
…

      They stare out to sea.
Sheesh. What a story.
Why is there no monument?
Huh?
You think there'd be a monument to commemorate something awful like that. Or to say sorry. Or something … I dunno.
We are the monument.
Markers of time.
Of stone
Of sand
And the metronome of the tide.
Gathering.
Remembering.

And every year,

On January 26th,
There are more of us.

Pronunciation guide
Please note that there are variations on the pronunciation and spelling of these words.
Budj Bim *Boodj-bim, 'boo' as in 'book' not 'boot'*
Gunditjmara *Goon-dich-mara, 'oo' as in 'book' not 'boot'*
Kilcarer gunditj *Kill-kara goon-dich, 'oo' as in 'book' not 'boot'*

Elders' Eyes

What would this look like through Elders' eyes?
They've felt the feelings,
Heard the sighs.

I'm yet to feel the highs and lows,
They've had them both
In ebbs and flows.

Their wisdom earned through paths they've walked
And with Ancestors
To whom they've talked.

The ones who've passed, I wish I'd known.
Their wisdom though
Can still be shown.

This problem now: so big, so wide,
I feel the need
To keep inside …

And yet the Elders' eyes and hearts
Could hold the answers,
In many parts.

I just need to open my ears,
To swallow my pride,
And squash my fears.

In letting go and opening up,
They might just fill
My cultural cup.

A story starts, a gentle ramble,
What is this?
… It's just preamble.

Before I know it, I see it plain.
They've found the source
Of all my pain,

But gently, and now here's the trick,
'This problem,
You can solve it quick.

You're not the first one to go through
This sticky spot—
I've been there too.

When you're out the other side,
I promise,
You won't need to hide.'

A whisper in my ear, a grin,
A slap on my back,
A smile on my chin.

Sage advice, swiftly delivered,
And yet as always,
So considered.

'Soon enough, there'll be laughs and fun,
Come on now,
You've got this son.'

Being Well

You know that word they toss around all the time?
Wellbeing.
Well,
It got me thinking
About where that word comes from …
I think.
A. Well. Being.
As in human being.
But why have we stripped the word human out of it?
Is being well just the absence of illness,
Or is it something much more?
Being well is stopping to inhale the eucalyptus, deep.
It's watching a fire burn down to cinders as darkness closes in.
Trailing your fingers through inky blue waters of a lake, seeing the ripple you created stretch across the surface.
Stamping the ground in ceremony.
Feeling the vibrations of a clapstick strike you in the bones.
Lingering to ask your Ancestors' advice on a sticky problem.
Celebrating the excellence of others, like screaming yourself hoarse at an Eddie Betts goal.
Eating a meal with your family, feeling nostalgic.
Cackling at a naughty joke.
Watching an autumn leaf make the choice to cut itself loose from its moorings and begin its tremulous, floating passage down to earth.
Being in an audience, all leaping to your feet together at the end of a special, shared experience.
Closing your eyes on a beach and hearing how loud the waves actually roar.
Gasping for air at the end of a hard, but good run.
Learning something new from someone you admire.

The truth is this.
Wellbeing is not a noun.
It's not possessed or lost.
It's not a lunchtime seminar on a stressful day.
Not a fad diet, or a side hustle, or a bursting bank balance.

Not something to be studied and regurgitated in an exam.
The clue is in the word.
Being—the verb.
A series of choices, experiences, memories, sensations,
From doing the being.
Well.

Photo: Tim Anastasi

Brodie Murray
Wamba Wamba and Ngarrindjeri

Discover the captivating theatre works of Brodie Murray, a proud Wamba Wamba and Ngarrindjeri man. With an authentic voice and a profound connection to his culture, Brodie's narratives are marked by their depth and emotional resonance, exploring themes such as survival, identity and the interplay between tradition and modernity.

Brodie would like to acknowledge that the following scripts were written on the lands of the Boonwurrung and Wurundjeri Woi Wurrung people of the Eastern Kulin Nation (Naarm/Melbourne) and the Djaara people of central Victoria (Castlemaine).

My River Country *Excerpts of monologue and text, set on Wamba Wamba Country, near Swan Hill, Victoria.*

WIRAN: I watch intently from the river red gums. Roots extend into the earth. Listen, listen to the hum of the earth. As the breeze blows gently from the east. Whispering. Whispering songs from another man's Country. Though the whisper is faint and far away. Waterways, songs. But from a different man's Country. Whose songlines run like veins through the land. Through theirs and into ours.

The heartbeat of the mother. As dusk slowly sets in. The Kurre gather at the bank, seeking refuge. They only want silence. They only want peace. They purse their lips, drinking from Mile. Ears pricked, listening for danger.

I watch closely as the boy rows his canoe. Ears pricked, deep listening. He rows across the great river. Body heaving, veins bulging. The mist rises above the cool water. Shielding the Pandyil swimming underneath the surface. The boy watches the bank. Eyes focused. The Kurre stand, watching the boy. But they do not move. They do not flinch.

For they know he has made the journey many times before. From dusk until the break of dawn. The weight of the canoe is heavy yet familiar. The rhythm of Mile, strong and grounding.

The young man reaches the bank. He crouches weary after a long day's journey. He scans his surroundings, eyes dilated. Breath quick and sharp. He crouches underfoot, like his Ancestors did. Listening to the land. It is in his blood. His storyline, his heritage. A warrior at heart. Though he may not know that yet.

> *The stars and constellations up above are reflected in the currents of the Mile. The sounds of bird calls from down river.*

The boy sits alone. On an old log which used to be a great river red gum. But something is different this time. His gaze is lowered, shoulders are sloped. I watch from my perch, here in the safety of the shade. The leaves cloak my presence, but I feel as though the boy can still feel that I am watching.

He gazes for a while. Head still lowered, breath slow and quiet. Not making a sound as others watch from the trees above. He stands legs firm. He lowers his arm, taking an object from the earth floor. The boy extends back his arm, launching it away. Letting out a piercing scream.

The sound radiates across Mile, birds and other animals fleeing in fear. But I stay and watch, as I am not afraid. As I feel his pain deeply.

The boy sits back down, as if all energy has left his own soul. He looks down again, lost on his journey. Regret brewing. Mistakes of the past.

As he looks back one last time, disappearing into the trees.

> *Dusk.* WIRAN *watches two* WARRIORS *who have been playing by the river. They eventually leaving the riverbank.* WIRAN *stays silent on her perch, as the river runs close by.*

Day turns to night. Night turns to a new day dawning. As I sit here on my perch. Silent yet intent. For I have seen one thousand moons. The knowledge of the stars and the earth. Above and below ground. The Creator Biarmi watches from the stars.

I can feel his presence. His mark on this land.

Night turns to day. Day turns to night. Boys together once again. The light of day shining through. Listen. Listen closely to that land. Leaves crunch underfoot. Mile rolling in the distance. As the Kurre drink as dusk sets in. Eyes watching from afar.

I am the protector. Watching over the boys as they sleep. Guiding them in their dreams. This is my story. This is our yarn from this Country. Wamba Wamba land.

> WIRAN *watches from afar. Watching silent and intently. Dusk sets in.*

I watch from the bank of Mile. Breeze whistles gently. Calling from the East. Messages and warnings sent far away from this Country.

The older boy sits restlessly by an old river red gum. Shoulders raised high and proud. Gaze distant and far away. For I have sensed this boy's presence before, in the depths of my memory. There is something different about him. He got no shame. Carrying himself high and proud like a Brolga.

Them frog necked owls call again from down river. Sending me messages from downstream. The boy stands, sinking his toes into wet earth. Grounding his stance into that land. Like tree roots extending into the land.

Others watch silently from the branches above. But he does not sense my presence nor theirs. Does not catch my gaze through the gum leaves. As I sit on my perch, launching into the night sky above.

> *Dusk. A branch of a river red gum close by to the river.* WIRAN *watches over. Silent. And observant. Ever present.*

I watch from the branches of an old river red gum. Roots extend into that earth. Listen. Listen to the gentle hum of the earth. As dusk approaches. The boy sits silent. I can feel his sadness. Eyes sunken, body loose.

He raises his gaze to the stars setting above. Casting Dreamtime stories across the night sky. What's he thinking? What does he want?

The Dreamtime plane up above. A land without sadness or hunger. A land without problems nor broken dreams. For the Dreamtime I have seen.

The boy stands. Casting his gaze closer to the riverbank. Eyes watching him from the shadows. The creatures of the night, and all Biarmi's creations. Frog necked owls call from down river.

He stretches his arms, taking a big yawn, heading into the hut. Sleep well young boy. Sleep well.

> *Late afternoon. Dusk sets in. The wind blowing gently from*

the east. WIRAN *watches intently from an old river red gum. Always watching. The warrior enters alone.*

I watch intently from an old river red gum. The breeze rustles the leaves, the whisper echoing again from far away. The boy enters, shoulders low to the earth. He looks up at the trees, perhaps feeling my presence. He hops in the canoe; body weary from a long day's journey.

The canoe sets off across Mile. The Kurre watch again, brown eyes reflecting knowledge. They do not fear him, do not fear his gaze across the waters. Kookaburras call as the eve of dusk sets in. Shadows dance like spirits across the earth floor. The sounds of the bush alive. Country alive.

The Pandyil lurk underneath the surface, eyes watching too. Waiting, waiting for the canoe to make its journey across the waters. The young man draws his gaze far away. As if worried for his journey ahead. For I have seen ten thousand moons. The knowledge of the stars and the earth.

He reaches the bank. Eyes tired and weary. He glances one last time across to the bank on the other side. Searching for something. Journeying into the bush and the night.

Pronunciation guide
Wamba Wamba: *Wham-Ba Wham-Ba, rhymes with Lamb-ba*
Mile: Murray River *Mill-ay, 'ay' as 'say'*
Kurre: Kangaroo *Koo-ray, rhymes with Hoo-ray*
Biarmi: Creator *Bee-army*
Pandyil: Fish/Murray cod *Poon-di, like 'book' not 'boot' and 'di' like 'me'*
Wiran: Red-tailed Black Cockatoo, spirit *Wir-an, 'Wir' rhymes with steer*

Yidaki / Didgeridoo

Deep listening. Gulpa Ngawal. Listening to the earth and surroundings.
Hear the Mile. Sounds of the currents and ripples.
Crouching underfoot like a warrior.
Toes sinking into wet earth. Listening to the earth.
The calls of pelicans close down river. The hum of Country all around.
Elders often speak about the sacred practice of deep listening.
When incorporating the sound of the yidaki and closing your eyes.
The sound travels as a vibration. Across the body and across Country.
  Remembering those night-time campfires in Balranald on Yanga Lake. The sounds of birds and wildlife.
I sit, amazed. Watching them play the didgeridoo and listening to music. Telling us about the sacred sites along the lake. Yarns passed down from father to fathers.
We hear about Bes Murray. Worked on Yanga station for 58 years. Old ways, survival. Sunsets and sunrise. The sounds of the yidaki are ancient. Back from the time of the dreaming.
It brings the old people close to us. Smells of the campfire, gum leaves and red-hot coals. Coals burning in the night. While we stared up at the night-time sky above. Constellations reflected in the ripples of Yanga Lake. I imagine generations ago when the Ancestors walked along the banks of Yanga Lake.
The Muthi Muthi mob. How pristine clear the lake was. A plentiful supply of freshwater fish and clams all year around.

The practice of Gulpa Ngawal cleanses our spirit.
Connects us from past to present. To our Ancestors and the spirits from the dreaming. Senses tuned to Country around me.
Deep listening is tuning in to the river, the open planes, the river red gums, the pelican flying on the other side of the river.
It is a part of our spirit if we choose to listen.

Pronunciation Guide
Muthi Muthi *Mutty-Mutty, gentle on the 'tt' almost Mudi-Mudi*
Yidaki *Yid-a-key*
Mile *mill-ay, 'ay' as in end of Ballet*
Gulpa Ngawal: deep listening *Gul-pa Na-wool*

The Marngrook

I close my eyes and tune in to the land around me.
Wamba Wamba Country. The Country around me.
Holding me closely.
Sun sets across Mile; casting distant ripples along the surface.
I hear echoes of the past. Children playing. Men and women laughing. Scent of gum leaves and roasting kangaroo meat. Taking me back hundreds of generations.
Back to the old ways. Old people.
In Victoria, the mobs created the game of AFL, called Marngrook. Young boys after a hunt. Early afternoon. They buried the possum skin, the Marngrook, in the dirt. Giving it back to Country. Back to the earth. Then they'd uncover it, bring it up from the ground. Ready to play the old game of Marngrook again.
Mobs would play it for hours on end. Sometimes even days. Bodies moving gracefully around the earth. Athletes moving in synchronicity. Dancing and connected to each other and the Country around them. Marngrook was and is the beginning of the game we now call AFL. Generations later.
I watch Bobby Hill move with a confidence and grace around the ground. On the biggest stages of the game. It's like he has a sixth sense. He just knows where the ball is going. Where it's been and where it's going to be. He's in tune with the land as well as the players around him.
Takes me back to the great Grand Final against the Lions. Bobby Hill against an unimaginable amount of pressure proved himself as best on ground to give the Pies the flag!
Bobby celebrates his goals with dance and movement. It is a magical experience just to witness his connection to both the game and his culture.
Takes me back to how the young fellas would have played Marngrook in Victoria. Back in the old times. Along the Mile (Murray River), young boys like Bobby anticipating the possum skin Marngrook. Catching it and spinning like Bobby Hill. Like a Leon Davis.
Leon Davis kicking a ridiculous snap goal from the boundary line on the biggest of stages at the MCG.

The MCG is on sacred ground, on the lands of the Wurundjeri people. On sacred land. Before the MCG was ever built, before white settlement. All the mobs of the Kulin Nations would have gathered in song and dance. Afterwards the young boys playing Marngrook.
Ceremony and ritual as old as time.
The Marngrook is something sacred. Something as old as time. Something which should be marvelled in this Country we call Australia. Something all Australians can respect and admire. Cherishing the great Aboriginal players of our game. Both past and present. The changemakers of this Nation. Pastor Sir Douglas Nicholls. Lance Franklin, Jamarra Ugle-Hagan and Leon Davis. Now the legendary Bobby Hill.
Think of them and think of their shared legacy and pride in their culture.
What can we learn about the game of Marngrook? Australia needs to acknowledge the game as the foundation of AFL.

Pronunciation Guide
Marngrook *from the Woiwurrung language of the Kulin nation, it is the name for traditional Indigenous Australian football. Marn-grook*

Good Works

Ron Murray is a Wamba Wamba wood sculptor, storyteller and artist. His practice centres around Koorie stories, community engagement. Amplifying our stories.
Stories of place and of Country and the stories which come from Country. The river mob. Our experiences.
He has been commissioned to create art pieces for people such as Muhammed Ali, Cat Stevens, Ash Barty and Sir Bob Geldof.
The practice of making a boomerang or didgeridoo is sacred and takes years to learn.
Memories take me back to when I was little following Dad in the mallee Country.
Walking through the bush looking for hollow trees.
Down at the bank of the Murray River looking for roots just above the surface.
The ones that had the right shape and bend were later crafted into bommerangs. One off each side. 'Brother and Sister boomerang' he would say.
Dad has passed down knowledge of story and culture.
Dad is using his practice as a knowledge holder. Keeping cultural practices alive. Educating wider society on Koorie ways of life.
Mentoring the boys in Youth Justice Centres, connecting them to their art, story and their Country.
Giving them the tools to use their arts practice for good.
Ron Murray is an artist.
                a storyteller.
                  a sculptor.

Representation

Where do you see yourself?
Do you see a space for you?
A place for you?

More mob. On big stages.
Hearing Koorie stories told in Victoria.
Their narratives, their way.
Stories from mobs across Victoria.
Wamba Wamba, Yorta Yorta,
Gunditjmara on the biggest stages.

Backing for representation.
Where are these stories shown?
Recognising the rich tapestry of First Nations stories.
Celebrating deep connection to performance, song.
Platforming these plays, songs, music on the biggest stages.

This is something we hope to see soon.

Thanks to community members, Elders …
Advocating for our voice, rights.

Keep telling these stories.

Reflections 1

Playing tennis with my brother. Feeling the flow.
Following his tennis career and success.
Seeing his connection to his identity and culture on the court.
Young mob—the future is bright.

Reflections 2

Writing for performance.
Creating and telling stories for the stage.
Writing a piece of poetry or spoken word.
Taking in Country all around.
The air, the earth. The animals and the trees.

Reflections 3

Family. Culture. Lore. Family is central.
Family is important.
Family shows us the way on our journey in life. Our journey in this world we live in each day.
Family grounds us to our identity.
To *our* culture and to our lore. Family. My brother, my friends. The First Peoples of this land. Stories, song lines, songs, place.
Those who believe in me. My friends.
Those who call a place home.
Those who will always call a place home.

Chorus presenting *CMT (Culturally Modified Tree)*.

Above: Lucy Gibson in *My Reincarnation*.
Below: Gilda Verner in *Life-long Friend*.

Above: Holly Allen, Sahana Rajarajan and Emmy McBride in *Conversation With Daughter.*
Below: Alice Guille in *Guide.*

Above: Luca Moutsos in *Wotjobaluk Stories*.
Below: Holly Allen and Riley Zhao in *Wotjobaluk Stories*.

Above: Taylor Warburton, Gilda Verner, Suriya Rajarajan and Samuel Licciardino in *United We Fall*.
Below: Lucy Gibson, Archie Baker, Kiara Gadd and Angel Li in *What Best Friends Do*.

Above: Lucy Gibson, Kiara Gadd and Suriya Rajarajan in *The Meeting*.
Below: Sahana Rajarajan and Chorus in *Pure Heart*.

Above: Arabella Walker in *The Hood*.
Below: Luca Moutsos, Ruby Molnar and Alexis King in *Fan (Stan)*.

Above: Roshni Sinha in *Haiku*.
Below: Alice Taberner in *Colours*.

Above: Chorus in *Concrete*.
Below: Riley Zhao and Archie Baker in *Papa*.

Above: Simon Liu and Samuel Licciardino in *Papa*.
Below: Alex Zhang and Chorus in *Echoes*.

Rungana Goverwa in *Elders' Eyes*.

Above: Charli Cowan in *Being Well*.
Below: Alexis King and chorus in *My River Country*.

Above: Zac Letts and Chorus in *Yidaki / Didgeridoo*.
Below: Chorus in *Marngrook*.

Ruby Molnar and Grace Wakeling in *Good Works*.

Above: Kiara Gadd and Chorus in *Representation*.
Below: Hamish Peatman and Antara Afra in *Reflections*.

Teachers' Notes

Tracey Rigney

CMT (Culturally Modified Tree)

This scene metaphorically explores the concept of cultural continuity and change through the lens of a tree that bears special scars—markings made by the First Nations peoples of Australia. These markings symbolise a deep connection to land, culture and ancestry. The chosen ones refer to trees selected for marking, symbolising individuals who carry forward the traditions and wisdom of their Ancestors. This scene reflects on the importance of maintaining cultural practices in the face of modern challenges and the loss of traditional knowledge.

Tips for Interpretation

Chorus Students form a living forest, with each representing a tree. They sway gently as they recite lines, symbolising the enduring presence of these marked trees through generations.

Monologue A single student, as the voice of a culturally modified tree, reflects on the history and significance of its scars, connecting the past with the present and future.

Movement Piece Students use dance and movement to represent the process of marking and the growth of trees, showing the cycle of life, tradition and memory.

My Reincarnation

In *My Reincarnation*, the speaker(s) navigates a surreal, dream-like landscape that intertwines elements of longing, loss and the cyclical nature of life and death. This scene suggests a deep yearning for connection with a lost love, manifesting through vivid, sometimes haunting, imagery. The progression from a cold desert to a cliff overlooking a turbulent sea and finally to a cemetery, represents the emotional journey of grief and the search for meaning after loss.

Tips for Interpretation

Chorus or Small Group A small group or chorus can act as the embodiment of the emotional landscape, narrating or commenting on the journey. They can use a combination of spoken word, vocal sounds and rhythmic movement to reflect the changing environments from the desert, to the cliff, to the sea and finally to the cemetery. This group could also represent the elements—wind, water, earth—interacting with the main speaker(s), creating a more immersive experience that conveys the speaker's internal and external journeys.

Monologue A student delivers a powerful monologue, embodying the speaker's journey through loss and longing, using tone and pace to convey the emotional landscape.

Duologue Two students represent the speaker and the imagined presence of the lost love, engaging in a dialogue that captures the essence of longing and the mirage of presence.

Creative Movement Through interpretive dance, students can portray the transition from the desert to the cliff and then to the cemetery, using their bodies to represent the shifting emotional states.

Life-long Friend

This scene portrays a poignant and imaginative exploration of grief as a life-long companion, beginning from a young age. Through a child's interaction with grief, personified as a new friend, the scene gently introduces the concept of loss and coping. The use of familiar, everyday settings and activities helps to demystify grief, presenting it as a natural part of life's experiences.

Tips for Interpretation

Duologue A student plays the child and another embodies grief, performing a dialogue that explores their evolving relationship through playful and reflective moments.

Choral Speaking A group of students could voice the child's internal monologue, with different voices representing different aspects of the child's emotions and experiences with grief.

Physical Theatre Through symbolic actions, such as hiding, climbing and observing, students can physically interpret the child's journey with grief, highlighting the emotional and physical spaces grief occupies.

Prop Use Use an apricot or a symbolic object to represent grief's presence and its impact on the child, with students interacting with the prop in various ways to signify key moments of the narrative.

Conversation with Daughter

Conversation with Daughter is a nostalgic script that vividly contrasts past and present ways of living, illustrating the dramatic changes in technology and childhood experiences. It captures a dialogue between a parent and a child, reminiscing about life before the digital era, filled with physical play and simpler forms of communication.

Tips for Interpretation

Duologue Students pair up to perform key exchanges from the script, focusing on the dialogue between the parent and the child about life before the internet. This fosters empathy and communication skills, encouraging students to engage with different viewpoints.

Creative Movement Students can use physical theatre to recreate scenes from the script, such as playing on pinball machines, riding bikes or jumping on trampolines. This helps students embody the physicality of a pre-digital childhood.

Choral Reading Perform a group recitation of the dialogue, emphasising the contrast between the parent's tone of nostalgia and the child's curiosity about the past. This highlights the generational differences in experiences and perceptions.

Tableau Vivant Create tableaux that capture key moments such as a family meal with no digital devices, playing outdoors or a classroom scene with vintage technology. This visually conveys the script's themes of nostalgia and change.

Small Group Scene Small groups enact scenes where they prepare for a day without digital technology, illustrating the steps of engaging in various outdoor and social activities. These scenes highlight the themes of teamwork, creativity and the shift from digital reliance to real-world interactions.

Guide

Guide is a spiritual and metaphorical journey through time, emphasising guidance, faith and connection. The imagery of a hand offering a white feather symbolises a gift of love and the promise of guidance through life's darkness and uncertainty. This scene invites contemplation of trust, the unknown and the strength found in companionship and guidance.

Tips for Interpretation

Creative Movement Students can use dance or movement to represent the journey, with one student guiding another, symbolising trust and guidance through physical space.

Choral Reading A group recitation, where the collective voice embodies the guide, offering strength and reassurance through the unified delivery of lines.

Symbolic Prop The white feather can be used as a central prop, passed among students to represent the sharing of guidance, love and support.

Tableau Vivant Create a series of still images or tableaux that capture key moments of the journey, using body language and facial expressions to convey emotion and narrative progress.

Wotjobaluk Stories: A trilogy as told by Tracey Rigney

This work could be a recurring motif within a larger work, intended to be interspersed throughout a theatrical performance or presented in sequence. Each section of the trilogy illuminates different facets of Wotjobaluk life, history and culture, providing audiences with a deeper understanding of the community's connection to the land, the impact of colonial history and the personal stories of its people.

Part 1: The Journey of Barringgi Gadyin

This scene traces the geographic and cultural journey of the Barringgi Gadyin, a river that flows through various terrains and holds deep cultural significance to the Wotjobaluk people. Students can explore the river's path from mountains to lakes, reflecting on how landscapes shape and are shaped by cultural narratives.

Part 2: The Legacy of Wotjobaluk Elders

This section reflects on the personal and communal histories related to the Barringgi Gadyin, through the stories of an Elder who witnessed the river's transformation and the impact of colonialism on the local community.

Part 3: Continuity and Change

The final section explores the generational transmission of culture and survival strategies, through stories of resilience and adaptation from the Elder's life and his Ancestors.

Tip for Interpretation

Storytelling, Movement and Songs Use a mix of storytelling, movement and songs to create a rich, multi-sensory experience that connects the audience with the story's cultural and emotional layers. Consider having multiple actors play the same character at different life stages or during different emotional states to provide varied perspectives and highlight the community's interconnectedness.

Digital Media for Context Use digital media to provide background information, additional narratives, or cultural context during the performance, making the experience more accessible and informative.

Dance and Movement Develop dance or movement sequences that symbolically represent the flow of the river, the growth of the community, or the impact of external forces, using body language to express themes not spoken aloud.

Chorus as Community Voice Incorporate a chorus that speaks for the community, providing historical commentary or cultural reflections that support the main narrative.

United We Fall

United We Fall is an evocative script that explores themes of rediscovery, joy and nurturing one's inner child through the playful and liberating act of roller skating. The script uses the imagery of skating equipment and the physical activity itself as metaphors for preparation and engagement in life's challenges and pleasures. It reflects on past neglect of one's playful side and celebrates the renewed connection and care for it. The narrative suggests a healing and strengthening of the self through fun, laughter and physical expression, highlighting the importance of self-compassion and joy.

Tips for Interpretation

Creative Movement Students can use dance or movement to represent the journey of rediscovering joy and freedom through roller skating, with one student guiding another, symbolising trust and support.

Monologue Students perform individual monologues reflecting on personal moments of neglecting and then reconnecting with aspects of their youth or simpler times, inspired by the script's narrative of rediscovery and affirmation of self-love.

Small Group Scene Small groups enact scenes where they prepare for a day of skating, illustrating the steps of gearing up and supporting each other in trying new tricks. These scenes highlight the themes of teamwork, support and the playful challenges of learning together.

What Best Friends Do ...

This scene is a heartfelt and humorous exploration of the unique bond shared between best friends. It highlights the small, intimate moments and shared experiences that define true friendship, from the mundane to the deeply meaningful. The narrative underscores the idea that best friends become chosen family, providing support, laughter and companionship through life's various ups and downs.

Tips for Interpretation

Duologue This could be a joyous, conversational exchange. Showcasing their chemistry and the nuances of best-friends relationship. The performers could explore a range of emotions, from the light-hearted and funny moments (like the toilet paper scenario) to the more profound and touching aspects of their bond (like sharing secrets and fears).

Choral Speaking A group of performers can deliver the lines in unison, emphasising the collective experience of friendship. Different voices can take turns narrating specific lines, creating a dynamic and engaging rhythm. The group can use synchronised gestures or movements to visually represent the actions described in the text, such as handing each other toilet paper or walking the cross-Country track together.

Creative Movement Performers can use movement to represent the various scenarios described. For instance, they can mime the act of texting each other, running the cross-Country track, or having a sleepover. The movements could highlight the physical closeness and support between the friends, showing how they move in harmony and support each other through different activities.

Tableau Vivant Create a series of tableaux that capture key moments described in the text. Each tableau can represent a different aspect of the friendship, such as laughing together, sharing secrets, or supporting each other. Use smooth transitions between the tableaux to show the passage of time and the evolving nature of the friendship, highlighting how it grows and strengthens over the years.

Group Scene Different pairs can take turns speaking different lines from the text, each representing a unique pair of best friends. This allows for a diverse representation of friendships and highlights the universal nature of the experiences described. The pairs can interact with each other, sharing knowing glances, laughs and gestures, creating a lively and interconnected portrayal of friendship. For instance, while one pair talks about texting each other all day, another pair can mime doing so in the background.

The Meeting

This scene presents a humorous yet profound dialogue that explores themes of acknowledgment, presence and the concept of apology within the context of a formal meeting. The repetitive questioning and play on words highlight the confusion and sometimes absurdity of bureaucratic procedures, while also touching on the importance of acknowledging traditional land ownership and the respect due to Ancestors and Elders.

Tips for Interpretation

Group Scene Set up the stage to represent a long table with many colleagues seated officiously, engaging in typical meeting behaviours (such as taking notes, nodding seriously). The disruption comes when one character starts questioning the process, causing shock and confusion among the colleagues. The colleagues could react dramatically to the disruption, looking aghast and whispering to each other, creating a humorous contrast between their serious demeanour and the unexpected questioning.

Duologue Cast one character as uptight and officious, adhering strictly to meeting protocols and procedures, while the other character is relaxed and nonchalant, causing friction and comedic tension. Use body language to enhance the comedy; the uptight character can be rigid and formal, while the relaxed character can slouch, put their feet up, or casually toss their notes aside.

Chorus Piece Have the chorus seated in a semicircle, all behaving uniformly, while one person stands out by doing something different (for example, asking questions, acting confused). The chorus could collectively turn to stare at them whenever they speak, exaggerating their reactions to emphasise the humour in the outsider's behaviour.

Tableau Vivant Create a series of tableaux that capture key moments in the dialogue, such as the initial acknowledgment, the questioning and the reactions. Each tableau could exaggerate the characters' emotions and reactions to enhance the comedic effect. Use exaggerated and dramatic transitions between tableaux to highlight the shift in tone and the growing confusion or frustration among the characters.

Pure Heart

This is a funny and touching script that addresses the superficiality of modern beauty standards and the importance of inner qualities like kindness and genuineness. The speaker offers a candid and impassioned plea to a younger person, urging them to embrace their natural self and not be swayed by the unrealistic portrayals often seen on social media and other platforms.

Tips for Interpretation

Duologue Pair the speaker with a younger character who is initially resistant and dismissive but gradually becomes more thoughtful and receptive. This interaction can highlight the generational differences and the impact of the advice given. The relaxed and genuine delivery of the speaker's lines could contrast with the younger character's initial eye-rolling and reluctance. The younger character's gradual change of heart can be depicted through body language and facial expressions.

Chorus Piece Use a chorus to deliver the monologue, with the group acting as a unified voice advocating for inner beauty and authenticity. The chorus can move and speak in sync to emphasise key points. Have one or two members of the chorus act out the role of the person being addressed, visibly reacting to the advice. This visual focus can draw attention to the impact of the message.

Prop Use Incorporate props like mirrors, make-up kits and social media icons. Use mirrors to symbolise self-reflection and the idea of inner beauty, while make-up kits can represent the superficial standards being criticised. Allow the audience to see the characters interact with these props, such as putting down a make-up brush in favour of looking into a mirror to reflect on their true self.

Tableau Vivant Create a series of tableaux that capture significant moments from the monologue, such as the speaker's passionate plea, the younger character's initial resistance and their eventual contemplation. Use exaggerated facial expressions and body language in the tableaux to highlight the emotional journey and the impact of the speaker's words.

The Hood

The Hood is a deeply introspective scene that explores themes of existentialism, identity and personal transformation. The narrative journeys through feelings of isolation and reflection in urban settings, contrasting them with profound connections to culture, home and relationships. It raises questions about the purpose of life, the nature of human experience and the ultimate search for meaning through personal growth and love.

Tips for Interpretation

Creative Movement Students can use interpretative dance or abstract movement to express the shifting emotions and journeys described in the poem. This could involve sequences that transition from isolation to discovery, representing the poem's shift from emptiness to fulfillment.

Chorus Reading Perform a group recitation of the scene, with different voices representing different stages of the narrator's life and emotional states. This collective delivery can enhance the poem's exploration of universal human experiences.

Symbolic Prop Use symbolic props such as masks or different pieces of clothing to represent the 'trying on personalities' and 'experimenting with bad habits' mentioned in the poem. These props can be used in a sequence where characters gradually shed them as they move towards self-discovery and connection.

Tableau Vivant Create a series of still images or tableaux that capture key moments of transformation and realisation in the poem. These can visually narrate the journey from feeling lost and alone to finding a sense of home and purpose through love.

Monologue Students perform individual monologues that delve into personal reflections inspired by the themes of the poem, such as what gives their lives meaning or a time they felt disconnected from their surroundings.

Small Group Scene Small groups can enact scenes that depict the poem's themes of searching and finding, such as a character journeying through different life stages and interactions, ultimately discovering a meaningful connection.

Duologue Students pair up to perform exchanges that might occur between the narrator and symbolic figures in their life, such as past selves or imagined futures, exploring the concept of unbecoming and becoming.

Fan (Stan)

Fan (Stan) captures the deep emotional connection and admiration for a music artist, seen through the lens of a lifelong fan. The poem explores themes of devotion, inspiration and the role of an artist as a pivotal presence throughout different phases of life—from childhood to adulthood. It delves into the transformative power of music and its ability to resonate through the highest highs and the lowest lows of life.

Tips for Interpretation

Use of Music Use recorded or live music to support your performance. You could use props such as headphones, or concert tickets as central items. These can be passed among students to symbolise the passing of musical influence and personal memories associated with specific songs or artists.

Tableau Vivant Create a series of still images or tableaux that capture key moments of musical influence, such as attending a concert, listening to music in solitude, or sharing songs with friends. These can visually narrate the poem's exploration of how music shapes personal and collective memories.

Monologue Students perform individual monologues that delve into their personal connections with music, perhaps reflecting on an artist or song that has significantly impacted their lives, inspired by the poem's theme of musical devotion.

Small Group Scene Small groups can enact scenes depicting different social settings where music plays a central role, such as a concert, a quiet listening session, or a lively discussion about favourite artists, illustrating the communal and individual aspects of musical experience.

January 26: Haiku

This haiku vividly encapsulates the initial encounter between Indigenous Australians and European settlers, using powerful imagery to reflect the dramatic and painful impact of colonisation.

When We Caste Our Eyes at Her: Haiku

This haiku challenges perceptions of Aboriginal identity with defiant humour, critiquing the superficial ways in which Indigenous identity is often recognised or acknowledged.

Referendum 2023: Haiku

This haiku captures the essence of Australia's 2023 referendum on Indigenous recognition. The poem succinctly reflects the nation's contemplation and the outcome of the vote, suggesting that a 'No' vote on the referendum not only speaks to Indigenous Australians' standing but also reflects the broader identity and values of the Australian people.

Tips for Interpretation

Chorus Use a choral arrangement where different voices echo the question 'what part of her is' with increasing intensity, followed by a unified, strong delivery of 'her middle finger?' This collective voice highlights community defiance against marginalisation and stereotyping.

Monologue A solo performer can interpret the haiku as a monologue that expresses personal defiance and pride in Aboriginal identity, using tone to convey a range of emotions from sarcasm to pride and resistance.

Poetic Reading Emphasise the lyrical quality of the haiku through a poetic reading that focuses on the rhythm and inherent defiance of the phrase 'her middle finger', pausing significantly before this line to draw attention to its impact.

Movement Piece Develop a movement sequence that embodies the tension and release of asserting Aboriginal identity against external perceptions. This could involve gestures of constriction followed by a bold, liberating gesture that matches the sentiment of 'her middle finger.'

Tom Molyneux

Colours

This scene reflects on the enduring and evolving relationship between the land and its people. The narrative traces the layers of a cliff, representing time, stories and cultural practices. It transitions from the historical and ceremonial use of natural pigments to a critical reflection on modern mapping and boundaries imposed by colonisation. The scene concludes with a young man connecting to his heritage through a ritualistic act, embodying the resilience and continuity of Indigenous culture.

Tips for Interpretation

Group Scene Use a group of actors to represent different layers of the cliff, with each actor symbolising a different time period or story. They can use their bodies and movements to create the visual of a layered cliff, coming together and shifting apart to show the passage of time and the changes imposed on the landscape. Incorporate choreographed movements that mimic the natural forces described (such as tides or landslides) to create a dynamic and engaging visual representation of the landscape's transformation over time.

Duologue Split the narration between an Elder (narrator) and a young man who performs the actions described in the scene. The Elder's reflective tone contrasts with the young man's purposeful and ritualistic actions, emphasising the connection between past and present.

Chorus Piece Use a chorus to deliver the narrative, with different voices taking turns to highlight various elements of the story. The chorus can collectively represent the community, echoing the historical and cultural significance of the cliff. The chorus can move in synchrony to create visual patterns that mimic the layers and colours described, using coordinated gestures to represent the transformation of the cliff into paint and canvas.

Tableau Vivant Create a series of tableaux to capture significant moments in the narrative, such as the description of the cliff's layers, the act of creating paint and the young man's ritualistic preparation. Use smooth transitions between tableaux to illustrate the flow of time and the continuity of cultural practices, emphasising the connection between past and present.

Monologue A single performer can deliver the text as a reflective monologue, emphasising the introspective and contemplative nature of the narrative. The performer should use varied tones and pacing to convey the depth of the cultural and historical reflections. The performer can use physical gestures and interactions with symbolic props to enhance the storytelling, creating a visceral and immersive experience for the audience.

Concrete

This scene is a powerful and symbolic representation of the struggle and resilience of the Aboriginal and Torres Strait Islander people. The performers, positioned in a semi-circle, engage in a rhythmic pounding of the earth, symbolising an attempt to break through an impossibly hard surface. The rhythms create a layered, dynamic effect that mirrors the ongoing struggle and persistence. The scene climaxes with an emotional shift as some performers transition to pounding their skulls and chests, embodying intense grief and struggle, before abruptly cutting out.

Tips for Interpretation

Group Scene Each performer could develop a distinct rhythm that interplays with the others, creating a complex and evolving soundscape. The rhythms could reflect the relentless effort and the synchronisation should mimic the natural, yet chaotic, patterns of struggle. Use various percussion instruments or body percussion to enhance the auditory experience. The performers can also incorporate stomping, clapping and other forms of rhythmic movement to add depth and intensity.

Emotional Shifts Highlight the emotional shifts by carefully timing when the performers transition from pounding the earth to pounding their skulls or chests. This could be done in a way that feels natural and deeply emotional, reflecting the personal and collective grief. Build the scene to a powerful crescendo with all performers fully engaged, then cut abruptly to silence. This sudden shift emphasises the futility and the weight of the struggle, leaving a profound impact on the audience.

Symbolic Gestures Use expressive body language to convey the effort, frustration and pain of the performers. The physicality of the pounding should be intense and deliberate, reflecting the impossibility of the task. Performers could use facial expressions to enhance the emotional depth of the scene, showing determination, sorrow and resolve.

Prop Use Incorporate natural elements like soil, stones and branches to enhance the visual symbolism. Performers can interact with these elements during the pounding, further emphasising the connection to the land. Keep the setting minimalistic to focus attention on the performers and their actions. The simplicity of the environment will highlight the intensity of the rhythmic pounding and the emotional shifts.

Lighting and Sound Use lighting to reflect the shifts in rhythm and emotion. Soft, warm lighting can create a sense of struggle and persistence, while harsher, colder lighting can emphasise moments of intense grief. Integrate subtle sound effects that complement the percussive rhythms, such as the sound of wind or distant thunder, to create an immersive atmosphere.

Papa

Papa is a moving script that delves into the poignant themes of memory, loss and familial connections. The narrative captures the complex relationship between a grandchild and their grandfather, who is grappling with dementia within the confines of an aged care facility. As the grandfather's memories become increasingly fragmented, the play explores the echoes of his past life, from being forcibly removed from his family as a child to his eventual reunion with his siblings. The dialogue between past and present in the script poignantly reflects on the impact of historical trauma and the bittersweet nature of recollection.

Tips for Interpretation

Choral Reading A group recitation can be used to emphasise the fragmented nature of memory. Different voices can represent different times in the grandfather's life, creating a layered narrative that reflects the complexity of his experiences.

Monologue Performers can deliver monologues that depict key moments of introspection from the grandchild or the grandfather. These can explore the emotional landscape of dealing with dementia, the pain of lost memories and the fleeting moments of clarity.

Duologue Key exchanges between the grandchild and the grandfather, or between the grandfather and his siblings, can be dramatised to highlight moments of connection and revelation. These scenes can focus on the struggle of communicating through the barrier of fading memory and the profound moments of recognition that occasionally pierce through.

Creative Movement Interpretative dance or abstract movement can be used to symbolise the shifting sands of memory and the emotional turmoil associated with dementia and historical trauma. Movements can be slow and disjointed, mirroring the frustration and confusion experienced by the characters.

Tableau Vivant Create a series of still images that capture the essence of key scenes—such as the grandfather being approached by the mysterious man or the emotional reunion with his brother. These tableaux can effectively convey powerful moments without the need for dialogue.

Small Group Scene Scenes involving interactions at the aged care facility or family gatherings can be performed by small groups to illustrate the dynamics of care, familial duty and the occasional chaos of collective memory.

Echoes

Echoes is a poignant exploration of the enduring connection between the present and the past, as symbolised by the timeless rhythm of the ocean waves. Through a series of conversations between unnamed characters, the piece delves into the layers of history embedded in the landscape, from ancient geological events to colonial encounters. The title *Echoes* reflects the recurring themes of memory, legacy and the cyclical nature of time, resonating across generations.

Tips for Interpretation

Physical Interpretation The chorus members could embody the elements of the landscape, with movements representing the ebb and flow of the tide, the formation of geological features like Budj Bim and the actions of historical figures such as the Kilcarer Gunditj and the Henty whalers. By physically embodying these elements, the chorus creates a vivid tableau of the land's history.

Soundscapes Incorporate sounds of the ocean, wind and wildlife to create an immersive auditory experience that complements the spoken text. The chorus members could also use their voices to mimic the sounds of nature, adding layers of texture to the performance.

Visual Imagery Utilise projected images or simple props to evoke key moments in the narrative, such as a silhouette of Budj Bim against a fiery sky or a representation of the Henty settlement on the beach. These visual cues help to contextualise the historical events and provide a visual anchor for the audience.

Narrative Framing Experiment with different ways of framing the conversations between the characters, such as overlapping dialogue, fragmented monologues, or poetic recitations. This non-linear approach reflects the fluidity of memory and the multiplicity of perspectives embedded in the land's history.

Elders' Eyes

Elders' Eyes is a reflective poem that delves into the profound wisdom and experience of Elders from the perspective of a younger generation. Through gentle dialogue and vivid imagery, the poem contrasts youthful uncertainty with the seasoned insights of those who have navigated life's challenges. It emphasises the importance of listening, learning and connecting with the past to find guidance and strength in the present.

Tips for Interpretation

Monologue A performer could deliver the poem as a monologue, embodying the introspective journey of the narrator. Use changes in tone and pacing to reflect the emotional shifts from uncertainty to revelation.

Choral Reading A group of performers can recite the poem, with different voices representing the narrator and the Elders. This can create a dynamic interplay between the youthful voice and the collective wisdom of the Elders.

Physical Theatre Use movement to represent the journey of understanding and connection. Performers can physically depict the 'paths' walked by the Elders and the act of 'opening up' to their wisdom, creating a visual metaphor for the poem's themes.

Symbolic Props Incorporate props such as a cup that the narrator fills as they receive wisdom, or objects representing the highs and lows of life, to visually enhance the narrative.

Soundscapes Integrate ambient sounds such as sighs, whispers and the gentle rustling of leaves to evoke the presence of the Elders and the ancestral connection. These sounds can underscore key moments in the poem.

Tableau Create a series of still images that capture significant moments in the poem, sharing wisdom, the narrator's realisation and the final, reassuring embrace. These tableaux can help convey the emotional depth and progression of the narrative.

Being Well

Being Well is a contemplative poem that examines the concept of wellbeing through sensory experiences and personal reflections. It challenges the conventional notion of wellbeing as merely the absence of illness, instead presenting it as a series of choices, experiences and sensations that enrich one's life. Through vivid imagery and evocative moments, the poem highlights the importance of being present and engaging with the world around us to truly achieve a state of wellness.

Tips for Interpretation

Monologue A performer could deliver the poem as a monologue, embodying the introspective journey of understanding wellbeing. Use changes in tone and pacing to reflect the various experiences and sensations described in the poem.

Choral Reading A group of performers can recite the poem, with different voices representing the different aspects of wellbeing. This can create a dynamic interplay between the various experiences and sensations described in the poem.

Physical Theatre Use movement to represent the sensory experiences and actions described in the poem. Performers can physically depict inhaling eucalyptus, watching a fire burn, trailing fingers through water and other moments, creating a visual metaphor for the poem's themes.

Symbolic Props Incorporate props such as eucalyptus leaves, a small fire pit, a bowl of water and other objects representing the sensory experiences described in the poem to visually enhance the narrative.

Soundscapes Integrate ambient sounds such as the crackling of a fire, the rustling of leaves, the sound of water and other sensory elements to evoke the experiences described in the poem. These sounds can underscore key moments in the poem.

Tableau Create a series of still images that capture significant moments in the poem, such as inhaling eucalyptus, watching a fire burn and trailing fingers through water. These tableaux can help convey the emotional depth and sensory richness of the narrative.

Brodie Murray

My River Country

My River Country is a poignant theatrical exploration set on Wamba Wamba land, near Swan Hill, Victoria. The narrative unfolds through a monologue that intertwines Wamba Wamba words with English, drawing deep connections between the land and its people. Wiran, embodied as a red-tailed black cockatoo, narrates the journey of a young boy as he navigates his heritage and the ancestral memories embedded in the landscape of the Murray River, or 'Mile'. Accompanying Wiran are other watchers who silently observe and guide, their presence a testament to the enduring connection between the physical and spiritual realms. These watchers add layers of depth and historical resonance, underscoring the narrative's connection to place and past.

Tips for Interpretation

Physical Embodiment Chorus members and actors embody the natural elements and spiritual essences mentioned in the script, such as the kangaroo ('Kurre'), Murray cod ('Pandyil') and the creator ('Biarmi'). Using expressive movement and symbolic gestures, they illustrate the integral roles these elements play in the narrative and their deeper symbolic meanings.

Soundscape Integrate natural sounds that resonate with Wamba Wamba Country, such as the flowing water of the Murray River, the calls of the red-tailed black cockatoo and the rustling of river red gums. This auditory backdrop enhances the sensory experience, grounding the audience in the setting and mood of the narrative.

Visual Imagery Use projected images of the riverine landscape, indigenous flora and fauna and celestial constellations to enrich the visual narrative. Employ symbolic props like a canoe or river stones to mark significant moments within the monologue, deepening the connection to the cultural and historical context.

Narrative Framing Experiment with a fragmented narrative structure to mirror the disjointed yet profound connection between past and present, memory and reality. This method allows the audience to experience the cyclical and layered nature of time and memory, much like the flow of the river itself.

Chorus Integration The chorus acts as the community and the land's voice, echoing the historical depth and emotional resonance of the narrative. They repeat key phrases or words in Wamba Wamba language, enhancing thematic resonance and providing a deeper cultural connection.

Small Group Work Small group scenes focus on interactions between elements like the river (Mile), the land and wildlife, discussing their roles and changes over time. This provides multiple perspectives and deeper insights into the narrative. Ancestral spirits may also appear, advising or reflecting on the current events, which helps contextualise the young boy's journey and decisions.

Yidaki / Didgeridoo

Yidaki / Didgeridoo explores the practice of deep listening, a sacred tradition among the Wamba Wamba people. This scene invites the audience to connect with the earth, the sounds of nature and the vibrations of the didgeridoo (yidaki). It emphasises the importance of listening to the environment, the wisdom of Elders and the timeless connection between people, land and Ancestors. The imagery of night-time campfires, the sounds of wildlife and the reflections on Yanga Lake evoke a profound sense of place and heritage.

Tips for Interpretation

Creative Movement Encourage students to use slow, deliberate movements to mimic the act of deep listening, with gestures that represent connecting with the earth and surroundings. Movements can illustrate the sinking of toes into wet earth, the calls of pelicans and the vibrations of the didgeridoo.

Soundscapes Incorporate natural sounds such as water ripples, bird calls and didgeridoo music to create an immersive auditory experience. Students can create these sounds using instruments or their voices, enhancing the atmosphere of the scene.

Symbolic Prop Use a didgeridoo as a central prop, allowing students to interact with it, symbolising the connection to their Ancestors and the earth. The prop can be passed among students to represent the sharing of cultural heritage and the continuity of tradition.

Tableau Vivant Create a series of still images or tableaux that capture key moments, such as sitting around the campfire, listening to the didgeridoo and reflecting by the lake. Use body language and facial expressions to convey the sense of wonder, reverence and connection to the land and Ancestors.

Choral Reading Perform a group recitation of the narrative, with students embodying the sounds of the Yidaki, the sounds of nature and the storyteller. The collective voice can enhance the sense of community and shared heritage, reinforcing the themes of deep listening and connection.

The Marngrook

The Marngrook takes us on a journey through Wamba Wamba Country, inviting us to tune into the land and the echoes of the past. This scene connects the traditional game of Marngrook, the precursor to modern AFL, with the present, highlighting the cultural significance and deep-rooted history of the game. The narrative follows the legacy of Marngrook, from the days of young boys playing with a possum skin ball to contemporary AFL stars like Bobby Hill, who embodies the spirit and grace of the game.

Tips for Interpretation

Creative Movement Students can use dance and movement to depict the flow and grace of Marngrook players, both past and present. Movements can illustrate the burying and uncovering of the Marngrook, the synchronicity of the players and the celebratory dances of modern players like Bobby Hill.

Soundscapes Incorporate sounds of nature such as rustling gum leaves, distant laughter and echoes of ancient times to create an immersive auditory experience. Use recordings of traditional Aboriginal music and didgeridoo to enhance the atmosphere and cultural connection.

Symbolic Prop Use a replica of the Marngrook (possum skin ball) as a central prop, allowing students to interact with it, symbolising the continuity of the game from ancient times to the present. The prop can be passed among students to represent the sharing of cultural heritage and the evolution of the game.

Tableau Vivant Create a series of still images or tableaux that capture key moments, such as young boys playing Marngrook, the ceremonial aspects of the game and modern AFL players in action. Use body language and facial expressions to convey the joy, pride and connection to the land and culture.

Choral Reading Perform a group recitation of the narrative, with students embodying the voices of the past and present, narrating the story of Marngrook and its significance. The collective voice, dispersed around the room like a crowd at the football could enhance the sense of continuity and shared heritage, reinforcing the themes of respect and admiration for the game and its players.

Good Works

Good Works is a reflective and insightful piece by Brodie Murray, focusing on the life and practice of Ron Murray, a Wamba Wamba wood sculptor, storyteller and artist. The narrative delves into the sacred process of creating boomerangs and didgeridoos, which takes years to master and is deeply rooted in the cultural heritage of the Koorie people. Ron Murray's work is a testament to the importance of preserving and sharing Koorie stories, engaging with the community and amplifying the voices and experiences of the river mob. Through his art, Ron has made significant contributions. His practice is not only about the creation of art but also about passing down cultural knowledge and traditions. This is exemplified in his mentorship of Aaron Nichols and the boys in Malmsbury Juvenile Justice, where he uses art to educate, connect and transform lives.

Tips for Interpretation

Creative Movement Performers can use movement to represent the process of searching for and selecting materials, mimicking the careful and sacred practice of choosing the right trees and roots. Movements can also depict the creation of boomerangs and didgeridoos, showing the transformation from raw materials to finished art pieces.

Symbolic Props Use props such as replica boomerangs and didgeridoos to symbolise the sacred art forms and their cultural significance. These props can be used in performances to highlight the craftsmanship and the stories embedded in each piece.

Tableau Vivant Create a series of still images or tableaux that capture key moments in Ron Murray's practice, such as searching for materials, creating art pieces and mentoring young people. Use body language and facial expressions to convey the reverence, dedication and cultural pride involved in the process.

Choral Reading Perform a group recitation of the narrative, with different performers voicing various aspects of Ron Murray's life and practice. The collective voice can enhance the themes of community, shared heritage and the continuity of cultural practices.

Representation

This scene calls for greater visibility and inclusion of First Nations stories on major stages in Australia. It explores themes of cultural identity, the importance of narrative and the need for recognition and support from the wider community. The piece is a powerful appeal for more representation and acknowledgment of the rich tapestry of First Nations stories, emphasising the role of community members and Elders in advocating for these voices.

Tips for Interpretation

Duologue A performer plays the narrator and another embodies the collective voices of First Nations communities, performing a dialogue that explores the call for representation and the acknowledgment of cultural stories on major stages.

Choral Speaking A group of performers could voice the hopes and demands of the First Nations communities, with different voices representing various tribes and their unique stories, creating a rich tapestry of voices seeking recognition.

Physical Theatre Through symbolic actions, such as reaching out, standing tall and embracing, performers can physically interpret the journey towards representation and the cultural connection to performance and song. Highlight the contrast between the current state and the hopeful future.

Prop Use Use symbolic props like traditional artifacts, cultural items, or a piece of fabric representing a tapestry, with performers interacting with the prop to signify key moments of the narrative and the richness of First Nations stories.

Reflections

Reflections is a series of introspective pieces that explore themes of identity, culture, family and personal journeys. Each reflection delves into different aspects of life, from the personal connection with a sibling's success in sports to the creative process of writing and the deep-rooted significance of family and culture. The overarching narrative ties together the importance of understanding and embracing one's heritage and the influence of loved ones on one's path.

Reflection 1 focuses on the bond between siblings, following a brother's tennis career and success and the connection to identity and culture through shared experiences and role models.

Reflection 2 delves into the creative process of writing for the stage, drawing inspiration from the natural surroundings and cultural heritage and expressing stories through poetry or spoken word.

Reflection 3 emphasises the central role of family in grounding one's identity and culture, highlighting the importance of familial support, cultural traditions and the sense of belonging within a community.

Tips for Interpretation

Creative Movement Performers can use movement to mimic playing tennis, highlighting the dynamic relationship and interaction between siblings.

Tableau Vivant Create a series of still images capturing key moments, such as training together, celebrating victories and moments of mentorship. Create still images depicting family gatherings, cultural rituals and moments of support and guidance.

Symbolic Props Incorporate items like notebooks, pens and elements from nature (leaves, stones) to symbolise the connection to the environment.

Choral Reading Perform a group recitation of the piece, with different performers emphasising various aspects of writing, nature and cultural storytelling.

www.currency.com.au

Visit Currency Press' website now to:
- Buy your books online
- Browse through our full list of titles, from plays to screenplays, books on theatre, film and music, and more
- Choose a play for your school or amateur performance group by cast size and gender
- Obtain information about performance rights
- Find out about theatre productions and other performing arts news across Australia
- For students, read our study guides
- For teachers, access syllabus and other relevant information
- Sign up for our email newsletter

The performing arts publisher

www.ingramcontent.com/pod-product-compliance
Lightning Source LLC
Chambersburg PA
CBHW040307170426
43194CB00022B/2931